AN UMBRELLA FROM PICCADILLY

AN UMBRELLA FROM PICCADILLY

by

JAROSLAV SEIFERT

Translated from the Czech by Ewald Osers

LONDON MAGAZINE EDITIONS

1983

For nothing this wide universe I call
Save thou, my rose

Shakespeare, Sonnets

*This book has been published
with financial assistance
from the Arts Council of Great Britain*

Published by London Magazine Editions
30 Thurloe Place, SW7
© Jaroslav Seifert
© Translation Ewald Osers
SBN 0904388-43-3

Printed by Unwin Brothers Limited
The Gresham Press
Old Woking, Surrey

Contents

Introduction	1
Autobiography	7
Silence Full of Sleighbells	9
The Hunt for the Kingfisher	13
A Garland on the Wrist	16
Finger Prints	18
November Rain	21
The Grave of Signor Casanova	24
Berthe Soucaret	27
Mácha's Nocturnal Journey to Prague	31
Prospect of Prague	34
The Song of the Whales	38
Mr Krösing's Top Hat	42
Lunar Ironmongery	44
The Head of the Virgin Mary	48
Four Small Windows	51
A Visit to the Painter Vladimír Komárek	55
An Umbrella from Piccadilly	57
The Struggle with the Angel	61
Fragment of a Letter	65
Window on Birds' Wings	68
The Mistress of the Poets	70
Lost Paradise	72
The Royal Pavilion	75
A Bowl of Nuts	79

INTRODUCTION

In Czechoslovakia, as in most of Eastern Europe, the writer – and, more particularly, the poet – is a public figure. People seem to care about their poets' views and ideas; they want to know where their poets stand on the great issues of the day. Even people who do not normally read poetry will be familiar with the major names. Whenever a new volume of poetry is published – and news about publication and distribution dates invariably seems to leak out – queues will form outside bookshops even before their doors open, and a couple of days later the new volume will have virtually disappeared from the shelves.

This position of the writer – not just in public esteem but in the hearts of the people – has its roots in the last century, when, throughout Central and Eastern Europe, the writers and intellectuals were in the forefront of national liberation struggles against autocratic, and usually foreign, rule and when, in many cases, they created or shaped the modern literary languages of that region.

Thus for nearly a century and a half the Czech writers, and especially the poets, have been 'the conscience of the nation'. During the tense days of 1938 the loudspeakers installed in the streets of Prague for the purpose of air-raid warnings and official instructions used their 'idle periods' to relay Czech poetry. After the Nazi invasion in 1939 and during the war the public, to show its contempt for the Nazi-controlled press, could be seen reading volumes of poetry in trams and buses. And the jittery brutality with which fascist and Stalinist regimes alike controlled, silenced and often jailed their writers is in itself evidence of their standing with the public.

One such figure is Jaroslav Seifert. Born in 1901, well-known and well-loved since his first volume, *City in Tears*, he has for

1

the past thirty years or so been universally acknowledged as the greatest living Czech poet.

The most astonishing thing about Seifert's popularity and reputation is that he has always been a shy, retiring person: he did not, like Nezval, march in the front rank of May Day processions; he did not, like so many of his contemporaries, give crowded public readings. But in some strange way, right from his first volume of poetry, he seemed to express, to echo, the feelings and the mood of his readers.

Seifert has never been a political poet – yet his work, for all its lyricism, musical quality and poetical power, has always been involved in the issues of his day. In the twenties and early thirties his engagement was on the side of the underdogs, of the poor, of those who had to live in the 'City in Tears'. Yet during the war, under the German occupation, his two long cycles, among the most luminous and beautiful poetry in the language, celebrated the splendour and magic of this same city, his native Prague, and – again without being 'political' in the normal meaning of the word – were a declaration of faith in the nation's final victory and resurgence.

Since the end of the war Seifert has repeatedly come into conflict with the regime – not for what he had written but for what, in the view of the administrators of culture, he had failed to write. Thus, during the years of Stalinist orthodoxy, he was accused of 'subjectivism' and of failing to see and write about 'the joy of the working man', his heroism and optimism. For a number of years, until 1954, Seifert was unable to publish any new poetry.

An important milestone in postwar Czech poetry was the Second Congress of the Czechoslovak Writers' Union in 1956, held under the impact of Khrushchev's famous condemnation of Stalin. The political leadership, throughout Eastern Europe, was still in a

2

state of disarray: there was uncertainty about the future direction of the official line, and the reins controlling the writers seemed temporarily to have slipped from the politicians' hands. Emboldened by this situation, and possibly intoxicated by what they perceived as the beginning of the Thaw, some of the writers at the Congress spoke out with a frankness not heard for nearly two decades. The poet František Hrubín referred to the 'unhealthy and degrading' situation in which Czech literature had found itself until then and compared the poet to the little boy in the Hans Christian Andersen story who alone uttered what everybody else knew: that the Emperor had no clothes. But Jaroslav Seifert went even further. For many years, he said, the writers had failed to fulfil their role of the conscience of the people. 'If an ordinary person is silent about the truth it may be a tactical manoeuvre. If a writer is silent he is lying . . .' Seifert spoke openly of the injustices done to writers and demanded that they be rectified. The cases of the imprisoned writers, he demanded, must be reviewed at once. It was a brave speech, one that is widely remembered to this day, but it achieved little. True, some hard-liners were voted off the Committee of the Writers' Union, and Hrubín and Seifert were elected to it. But the Congress had opened a gulf between the writers and the political leaders; the writers – in the words of A. French's excellent analysis* – had 'crossed over from the protection of the official ranks to the people, abandoning their patron for their audience'. For Seifert, personally, his attack on the official concept of the new socialist literature and his only half-veiled suggestion of guilt in high places meant that, for a number of years, although his past work was being republished in five volumes, no new poetry by him appeared.

In 1968 Seifert came out openly against the Soviet intervention in Czechoslovakia, but in 1969 – realignment to the new policy

* A. French: *Czech Writers and Politics* 1945-1969 (Australian National University Press, Canberra 1982).

proceeded slowly – he was elected President of the Czechoslovak Writers' Union, the last President before its dissolution. (The Union has since been re-established on a new pattern but Seifert has so far declined to join it.)

There followed a strange period of twilight. His pre-1968 poetry was published in collected form but his new poetry, *The Plague Column* (1977) and *An Umbrella from Piccadilly* (1980), had to appear in (lovingly and endlessly typed and retyped) *samizdat* form. Ultimately – perhaps because his position in the hearts of his people was too firmly and deeply rooted, or perhaps because of a more liberal attitude on the part of the authorities, both these volumes were officially published in Prague in 1981, and a further volume, *To Be a Poet*, is to be published shortly. On his 80th birthday, in the autumn of 1981, Seifert received the public congratulations of President and First Secretary Gustav Husák and of other political leaders, and a tribute (though not entirely free from reservations) appeared in *Rudé Právo*.

It is difficult to be sure about the reasons for Seifert's enormous popularity with Czech readers of all age groups: my own feeling is that his power lies in the immediacy and human warmth of his writing. He has now dispensed with the superb technical mastery – 'verbal wizardry' would not be too strong a description – he displayed in his wartime cycle *Robed in Light*. He uses simple, at times colloquial and popular, language but he handles it with a sureness and precision that lend his 'free' verse an inner rhythm and crispness. It is the startling nature of his images, the way they contrast with each other and with the simplicity of his diction, that give rise to the poetry.

It is worth reminding oneself that this volume was written when Seifert was 79. Of course it is retrospective and, most of the time, nostalgic. But it has nothing of the elderly slippered domesticity of late Auden or the religious introspection of late Eliot. This is the full-blooded poetry of a man who has loved life, women, and love itself.

4

Seifert, at 81, is in poor physical health. But he still astonishes and charms his visitor with his mental liveliness, his sense of humour and his insatiable intellectual curiosity. One must hope that this major Czech poet will now be able to live out his life unharassed: writing, seeing his work published, and receiving the recognition due to him.

E.O.

AUTOBIOGRAPHY

Sometimes,
when she would talk about herself,
my mother said:
My life was sad and quiet,
I always walked on tip-toe.
But if I got a little angry
and stamped my foot
the cups, which had been my mother's,
would tinkle on the dresser
and make me laugh.

At the moment of my birth, so I am told,
a butterfly flew in by the window
and settled on my mother's bed,
but that same moment a dog howled in the yard.
My mother thought it
a bad omen.

My life of course has not been quite
as peaceful as hers.
But if I gaze upon our present days
with wistfulness
as if at empty picture frames
and all I see is a dusty wall,
it has been so beautiful.

There are many moments
I cannot forget,
moments like radiant flowers
in all possible colours and hues,
while evenings filled with fragrance
resembled purple grapes
hidden in the leaves of darkness.

With passion I read poetry
and loved music
and blundered, ever surprised,
from beauty to beauty.
But when I first saw
the picture of a nude woman
I began to believe in miracles.

My life unrolled swiftly.
It was too short
for my vast longings
which had no bounds.
Before I knew it
my life's end was drawing near

Death soon will kick open my door
and enter.
With startled terror at that minute
I'll catch my breath
and forget to breathe again.

May I not be denied the time
once more to kiss the hands
of her who patiently and with my steps
walked on and on and on
and loved me most.

SILENCE FULL OF SLEIGHBELLS

How the evenings are drawing in,
mother would complain,
go light the lamp!
The flame, sooty at first,
lit up a little cloud of smoke
from father's pipe.
Smokers don't enjoy smoking in the dark.
So we began to talk
of this and that.
All night through snow was falling.

In Prague you could still come across
old-fashioned horse-sleighs.
They were the last of their kind in the city.
They carried a silence
full of gentle sleighbells
from somewhere in past centuries.

How pleasant it would have been
to huddle into soft blankets.
I'd squeeze your hand
and put my arm round your shoulders.
Your breath would soon have hung
on the whiskers of the fur
like nuptial silver threads of frost.

As we were walking to the viewing tower
past benches deep in snow
the wind gusted fiercely
and soon the shameless frost
got under our fingernails.

As for my gloves, I'd leave those in my pocket.
But then you know!
In rubber gloves it's difficult to hold
even ordinary crockery,
let alone tea cups
with a small Meissen rose inside.

They're smooth
and of such amorous shape
that as you lift them in your fingers
they tremble in your grip.

Luckily there are still moments
when even in winter you don't freeze
and you don't have to think of anything
except
what you are longing for.
And you'll sit on that snow-covered seat
as if it were a fragrant patch of grass
with clumps of daisies.

10

Although there was a frost that time,
and snow was falling,
around your mouth spring had already come
and your lips gently trembled,
one moment with tenderness,
one moment with rose-coloured confusion,
one moment with fear,
and God knows what else.

Alas that everything that lives
and fiercely blooms
should last a short time only.
And meanwhile the years fall back beneath you
like the rungs of a gardener's ladder
which you are climbing.
And when you've stepped on the last rung
to pick the last apple
you'll break your neck.

What has become of you
in those few years?
Time is not overfond of everlasting love.
Maybe we've actually caught sight of one another
somewhere since then.
But I'm an old man now
and you no longer recognized me.

Maybe we've even met
but in embarrassment
each looked another way
as if we'd never seen each other
in all our lives.
That too can happen.

Even so from time to time
Monsieur Neruda would
encounter Madame Karolína Světlá
in King Charles Square.
Monsieur Neruda did not raise his hat
and Madame Karolína Světlá
stared at the ground.

THE HUNT FOR THE KINGFISHER

How many time has not a verse come to my mind
even at the crossroads
while the lights were at red!
Why not?
You can even fall in love
in that short time.

But before I'd crossed over
to the far side
I'd forgotten the verses.
Then I was still able
to shake them out of my sleeve.
But the smile
of the girl who crossed over in front of me
I remember to this day.

Under the railway bridge at Kralupy
I often as a boy would climb
into the branches of a hollow willow
and among the twigs above the river
would think and dream
of my first verses.

But, to be honest, I also
would think and dream
of love and women
and watch the torn-off reeds
float on the water.

Easter was round the corner,
the air was full of vernal magic.
I even saw a kingfisher once
on a whipping twig.

In all my life
I never saw another
and yet my eyes have often longed
to see that delicate beauty closer.

Even the river had a pungent fragrance then,
that bitter-sweet fragrance,
the fragrance of women's loosened hair
when from their shoulders it overflows
their naked bodies.

And when, years later, I immersed
my face into that hair
and opened my eyes,
I gazed through those sunlit depths
to the roots of love.

At times there are moments in my life
when I find myself once more
under the railway bridge at Kralupy.
Everything there is as it used to be,
even that willow –
but I am just imagining it all.

Easter is once more round the corner,
the air is full of vernal magic
and the river is fragrant.

For everyday under my window
the birds go mad quite early in the morning
and, singing as if their lives depended on it,
they drown each other's voices,
and those sweet dreams
which usually only come at dawn
are gone.

But that's the only thing
I can reproach spring for.

A GARLAND ON THE WRIST

I too, on Corpus Christi Day,
used to inhale the fragrance of incense
and thread a garland on my wrist
of fresh spring flowers.
I too used to gaze up towards the sky
devoutly, listening to the bells.
I thought that was enough
but it wasn't.

How often has a fugitive spring
with its heel stirred up a flurry of blossom
under my window,
and long ago I realized
that a fragrant bloom
and a woman's body radiating nakedness
are two things
more beautiful than anything else
on this miserable earth.

Bloom and bloom,
two blooms so close to each other.

But life escaped me hurriedly
like water through my fingers,
even before
I'd managed to assuage my thirst . . .

Where are those garlands of spring blossom!
Today, as I hear the creak
of the death chamber's door,
when I've nothing left to believe in
except something too much akin to nothing,
when the blood is pounding in my veins
like the condemned man's drum,
when all that remains is the stereotype
of human ruin
and all hope is as worthless
as the old collar
of a dead and mangy dog,
I sleep badly at night.

And that is how I heard
someone tap softly
on my half-closed window.

It was just a branch of the tree
flowering in spring,
and my two sticks
with which I drag myself about
day after day
did not for once have to transform themselves
into a pair of wings.

FINGER PRINTS

Even by force I make the night surrender
pleasant dreams.
Alas, mostly in vain.
But life, at least, allows us
to return against the current of time
not without vertigo, but with some slight regret
and a tear of sadness,
all the way
to where our memory reaches.

Remembrances, however, have a woman's skin.
When you taste them with the tip of your tongue
they taste sweet
and have an exciting fragrance.
So what!

The statue of the Vltava river by Václav Pachner
in the façade of the Clam-Gallas palace
pours from its jug
a stream of water
intertwined with stars.
She has long bewitched my eyes
with her shapely nudity.

Confused they strayed a long time
over her body,
not knowing where to settle first.
On her delightful face
or on the virgin charms
of her lily-of-the-valley breasts
which so often are the crown
of all the beauty of the female form
in all parts of the world.

I must have been fourteen,
or maybe a year older,
as I stood there bewildered,
as if waiting
for her to raise her eyes to me
and smile.

One moment when I thought
no one was watching
I managed, from the basin's edge,
to clasp her leg in my palm.
Higher I didn't get.
It was rough, it was made of sandstone,
and it was cold.
It was still snowing lightly.
But a hot wave of desire
like an electric shock
surged through my blood.

But if love is something more
than a mere touch,
and it is that,
a drop of dew can sometimes be enough,
suddenly trickling down on to your hand
from a flower petal.
Your head suddenly spins
as if your thirsty lips had gulped
some heavy wine.

In the doorway of the Clementinum nearby
stood a policeman.
And while the wind was ruffling
the cock's tail feather on his hat
he looked around.

He could have easily run me in.
No doubt I'd left my finger prints
on the girl's calf.
Perhaps I had committed an offence
against public morality,
I don't know!
I know nothing about the law.
Yet I was sentenced after all
to lifelong punishment.

If love is a labyrinth
full of glittering mirrors,
and it is that,
I'd crossed its threshold
and entered.

And from the bewitching glitter of mirrors
I haven't found the way out
to this day.

20

NOVEMBER RAIN

How vulnerable a sleeper is at night!
When he's attacked
by cruel and senseless dreams
he calls for help in his sleep.
And yet these are just worthless coins
in a pocket with holes in.

I do not like those noctural incidents
when darkness begins to relate
yesterday's adventures.
Dreams hurtle from darkness into shadows,
they can't stand up to daylight.
No hand controls their reins,
the halter-bells don't tinkle.
They're mute.

Those dreams with half-closed eyes
are happier.
I can summon up whomsoever I wish,
even those who left us long ago
and whom I loved.
They willingly come to me
and prolong their lives
by those few moments.

It was raining, it was November.
I was sitting in the train, on my way to the cemetery
to visit my dead.
The drops were shattering against the window
and the glass was like a ruffled mirror.
And smiling at me, from its surface, was
a girl's face.

– Why, I have almost forgotten you
and you still smile at me?
– I've long ceased to be jealous of anyone
and I have long disdained all hope.
You see me as a young girl, just like then,
I'm dead but I'm not getting any older.
I no longer exist, and I am nothing,
all I can give you now is a sweet memory.
It may inflame you like a sip of wine
but won't intoxicate.
And no hangover either.

– Do you still remember?
I read your verses late into the night.
Sometimes the crowing of the cock
sent me to bed.

– And I have dropped all shame:
I come to meet you of my own intent
and I myself unbutton my bodice.
Embrace me.
Even the dead have need of a little love
when they've so far to walk
to the very end of eternity.

– If you still think of me sometime
write me a few verses.
I'm curious.

The train was pulling into the station
and the girl's face was lost to me
among the drops on the window.
As I was leaving the station concourse
I didn't look where I was going
and people bumped into me.
But two days later I was whispering these verses
into the dead locks on her temple.

THE GRAVE OF SIGNOR CASANOVA

In the days when life seemed a dream
and yet wasn't a dream,
when we foolishly believed
that days were created for smiles
and evenings for love,
a girl with golden hair said to me:

– Goodbye! And I don't want
this flower you gave me any more.
Put it on the grave of that libertine,
that violator of virgins
who were then still devoutly guarding
their hot secret
in a gently closed lap,
that seducer of virtuous women,
about whom you've been telling me
oh so touchingly.

I too said goodbye to her
and with a handshake
promised to do so.

The storms upon my sky have long stopped roaring,
the lightning has died down
like candles in a chandelier at a ball.
My hair now is whiter
than the ermine of the copes
enveloping the Canons
of St. Vitus' Chapter
when they sit down on their wooden seats
on winter evenings.

I had not forgotten my promise,
even though a good number of years
had galloped past in their costumes
to even older costumes,
and one day I was going to the town
in Northern Bohemia,
where the roses smell of coal smoke
and where your teeth grit
not on salt or sand
but on black dust.

The girl had long been dead.
She'd died quite young
and scarcely had known love.
She was lying on her gleaming bunch of hair
like a saint
and on her maiden breasts,
like two inverted water-lily blooms,
only a little wilted,
she held a half-open fan
of rose-red gossamer.
And she was deader
than the severed wing of a swan
killed somewhere in the Royal Deerpark.

Signor Giovanni Giacomo Casanova
de Seingalt
was buried at Duchcov,
somewhere near the cemetery wall
by the chapel of Saint Barbara.
The cemetery has been pulled down
and the grave levelled with the ground.

All that is left of the famous adventures
of Signor Casanova
is the grey colour of the long roads,
and of all his loves
just a spring breeze.

His dust, however, has seeped deep
into Bohemia's soil,
far from the city of Venice
which he loved.

What is there to be added to this story?
Hardly anything.
Except perhaps that all our lives
are merely one laborious, painful search
for our own graves.

BERTHE SOUCARET

When Berthe Soucaret,
an unknown Creole girl from Guadalupe,
was eighteen
she was elected beauty queen.

She was the first queen in the world
and all women
at once looked at their mirrors.

That was at Spa in Belgium,
that town of bubbles, flowers and of song,
on 18th September 1888.
On a dust-covered music box,
dug up among some junk in the attic,
I found the same year marked
in golden figures.
The music box played one of the love songs
of Franz Schubert.

A lot of years had passed
since her coronation
and she had long been dead
when I fell in love
with her shadow
I had encountered in my youth.
From that moment I have sought that beauty
in the features of those
towards whom I was running.

Why cannot every woman –
at least some time, at least for a while,
at least for one pair of eyes –
be the most beautiful woman in the world?

Fingers straying over the body's firmament
like stars over the sky,
until her whole body flares up
with the flame burning within.
Lips drinking from lips
and thirst is not assuaged
and longing for delight leads both of them
to the ancient ritual.

What more beautiful gift has life to give
than love?
Garlanded with the green boughs
of its earthliness
it is nearest to heaven
and it alone offers a glimpse
of how happy we should probably be
if only –

Soon the woman brushes all the kisses
from her burning face
and with both hands
reaches up to her loosened hair
to hold back for a short while
the fugitive gleam of her crown.

One girl will come, and then another
after many years.
In the flowered dress of memories
she will rustle with words so soft
I can hardly hear them.
But presently they disappear again,
one after another,
and I must bury them again
in the nocturnal darkness,
back to the darkness whence they came
and that is even blacker!
No longer tears, no longer a torch,
and maybe forever.

Among those who came was Berthe Soucaret,
the young Creole girl from the island of Guadalupe
which smells of vanilla.
Maybe she was the most beautiful of all.
Maybe. I don't remember.

Don't go away just yet
and do believe me:
I had to fall upon my knees
before your beauty then,
and only in my dream I kissed
its feet,
even though you were already dead.

Whenever I remember you
to this day
I hear my old heart beating.

As for those memories which were not pleasant
and those which had no love,
I've left them lying by the road,
a prey to condors.

MÁCHA'S NOCTURNAL JOURNEY TO PRAGUE

'During the night from Saturday to Sunday Mácha set out from Litoměřice to Prague.'

Karel Janský

He strode on hurriedly:
Under the whip of longing
he walked with his head erect:
Longing to him was as wings to a bird.
He dreamed and raged.
Along the road the dogs were barking at him.
But he was accustomed to the bark of dogs
from back in Prague.

Ceaselessly he was thinking of Lori
She often cried.
But he was not a man to be upset
by woman's tears.
Now she was crying, nursing her little son.

He dearly loved the child.
He shared with him the woman's love
and he would smile
whenever the boy was trying to get hold of
her nipples.

Love was lighting his way.
The white milestones along the road
quickly dropped into the darkness behind him
like the ever new images
of the girl's body
in his insatiable eyes.

In his hands and in his teeth
he always tried to capture
that brief moment of panting passion,
before he laid his feverish face
into the woman's hair as though
into a flaming halo
and slowly inhaled into his nostrils
the intimate fragrance.

All his life
he'd ruthlessly, if need be by her hair,
drag his wife
always to him alone and after him
and always upward.

He bullied her and threatened
and all the time he trembled full of love,
he clenched his fists
and choked with gentleness.

But if he were to die
– that, too, could happen –
Lori would open a haberdashery shop.
O Lord! The thought alarmed him.

Ahead of him on the distant skyline
was St. Vitus' Cathedral.
The pale light of the moon
scarcely revealed its silhouette.
Kings of Bohemia, stand by him!
He too is a king.

The pane vibrated
as the bell rattled
and someone called out in a sleepy voice.
He shouted angrily: Open up!
Hurry up and open, this is me!

He drew a painful breath.
But love was here to meet him with
wide-open arms.

PROSPECT OF PRAGUE

Once upon a time – the ancient story-tellers
used to begin thus –
I was returning home along the river.
The river was calm and quiet
and in the silence I could hear the murmur
of flowing time
in the bottom of the hour-glass.
The older you get the better you hear
that sound of time.

The houses are mirrored in the water,
roofs downward,
and their outlines are trembling.
Their windows have been glazed only with water
and only a mermaid could inhabit
their flickering shadows.

I knew a mermaid
years ago, as a young boy.

Into the gentle lap of a young woman,
more beautiful than the princess in the castle,
she once laid an apple.
No painter could have painted one so beautiful.
   Under its sweet peel
there were all kinds of magic:
the magic of love, the magic of pleasure and passion,
the magic of longing
and the magic of the moment when one person gives
himself to the person he loves.

The talking bird in its golden cage
turned to her startled face
and screamed at her:
                            – That'll teach you!
Faced with that precious gift the girl
burst into tears.

She thought love knew no boundaries
and lasted
as the sun or the stars in the sky,
but of the men she encountered
none had enough courage
to repay her in like coin . . .

One in no time gave her only pain,
another grief
and nights of tears,
or just cold nothingness . . .
But always for a big armful of love.
As soon as it heard her bitter lament
the talking bird in its golden cage
screamed into the dark:
                            – That'll teach you!
She heard him but it was too late.

At the time when in the Prague she loved
she was only vegetating,
she was sick and all her beauty gone,
the painter Morstadt was still busy drawing
his prospects
full of light and comfort and of peace.

Look, two gentlemen are here escorting
a lady dressed in pink.
That which glistens high above their heads,
Prague's ancient Castle and St. Vitus' Cathedral,
is the crown
on the royal brow of the city.

At first glance one might get the impression
that life was happier in those days.
It's a delusion.
Neither was life happy in those days,
nor were the towers quite as high
as the painter made them.
The engravings merely try to force upon us
a beautiful lie.

It is over a hundred years
since they brought Mme Němcová back
from Litomyšl.
She was sick and death was fast approaching,
death indeed already sat on her tongue.
Someone's hand tried to reverse
the clock of her life.
But the sands were finally running out,
her time was up.

With tears in her beautiful eyes
Karolína Světlá put on
a black brocade dress with a lace.
How it suited her!
Neruda was quite bowled over,
could not take his eyes off her.

As the cortège moved off from the Three Lindens
in Příkopy Street
the talking bird in its golden cage
turned to the dead woman
and, as the black hearse itself moved off,
screamed after her, one last time:
                              – That'll teach you!

THE SONG OF THE WHALES

I only roamed a few days
in the south of France
but to this day I hear the crash of the waves
against the rocky shore.

My first glimpse of the sea
was from the platform of a railway carriage.
It took my breath away
and from surprise
I was incapable of speech.

The mimosas had long faded
but their sweet scent
still permeated the scorched earth.
But when in my cupped hands I tasted
the water of the sea
it was not as bitter
as human tears.

How did I know?
I used to kiss your face
when you cried.

It was that most delightful time
when the tree of our lives
began to bloom.
Seconds, hours and pleasurable days
were flying before me
like butterflies
and my head was aflame.
But in my life I suffered no other pains
than love.

Teige and I were making for Paris
by a round-about route.
Paris was buzzing with new poetry
and colours were erupting
whenever a brush touched canvas.
We then believed
that one could live in Paris only
and nowhere else.

I hastily caressed the sea with my eyes,
a little ungratefully
we bade the waves good-night —
as if the waves could ever sleep!
I have regretted it ever since
and frequently have asked the sea's forgiveness.

I thought that there were greater mysteries
than those hidden by the sea.
Paris was full of them.
Human hearts, roses and violins
all keep their own
whereas the poet in his pocket has the key
to everything on earth:
he knows the mystery of love.
We spent some time at the Louvre
and some time elsewhere,
some minutes in a suburban dancing place,
where we drank absinth,
a little while in the cemetery.

And youth,
without fanfares,
without the sobbing chords of harps,
without tears
and without a triumphal arch,
was gone.

Thereafter life merely raced ahead,
not worth a broken farthing.
Better not think of it.

Be quiet now, don't lie,
and just remember!

But I soon secretly began
to hate even Paris.
With the madness of America's great cities
she was, year after year,
losing a little of her coquettish old-fashioned flavour
and becoming different.

Yet over the sea time hung
still as a star.
The waves clash ceaselessly against the rocks,
and if Knüpfer's naiads
were still sunbathing on those rocks
they would not show a wrinkle
even in a hundred years.

Mr Roger Payne and his wife Kathy
understood the language of the whales
and off the Hawaian islands and Bermuda
recorded the song of the whalebone whales
which the sailors call
humpbacks.

The whales today are near extinction.
Theirs could well be a funeral song.
But it is not!
In those dusky depths of the sea
it sounds solemn.

Perhaps we should stand up
and doff our hats
and stand straight to attention
light lighthouses.

Perhaps this is the Anthem of the Sea!
It rings out rarely
but it has done since the beginning of time.

MR KRÖSING'S TOP HAT

There was a time when Prague
among all the cities of Europe,
such as London, Rome and Paris,
was poor enough to make you cry.
What did it have, when all was said, except the Castle?
A flight of doves on St. Nicholas's belfry,
a Viewing Tower
and sour grapes in the Gröber Park.

Paris was all the rage.

Prague with its geraniums in the windows
and modest net curtains
of cheap material
was quiet and sweet as the blossom
of a wild rose.

A tall top hat then used to walk
along the Embankment.
It belonged to Mr Krösing,
a singer from the National Theatre.

It was a somewhat strange hat
and I think it was unique in Prague.
Except, perhaps, in theatrical wardrobes.

It was reminiscent of those famous top hats
of great conjurers
whose subtle fingers would produce from them
a multitude of silken scarves,
a little the worse for wear,
and finally, flying up from it,
six frightened doves.

Suddenly the top hat was gone
and a black flag flew from the National Theatre.

Meanwhile on Petřín Hill there was a spot of rain,
the rain was rose-coloured and smelled of young girls' lips
and fell caressingly into a young lap
where but a few moments earlier had lain,
as though severed,
a young man's tousled head.

Maybe that time it was my own,
I don't recall; it was too long ago.

Prague was gazing out of all its windows,
smiling happily
at herself.

Across the road in the Café Slavia
Karel Teige had the night before cut up
some crêpe-de-chine to make a spring dress
for young poetry.

Au revoir! Or rather: good night!
It was so long ago, my dear.

LUNAR IRONMONGERY

Of love, perhaps, or perhaps of women
one might talk at greater length –
but our talks of poetry,
of the beauty of verses,
of the mystery of words,
were likewise endless,
good Lord!

Night would begin to pale,
the impatient dew would fall
sometimes when I accompanied
the poet Hora
along that long Plzeňská Road
to Košíře.

When we passed the Little City cemetery,
where death has now long ceased to live,
the graveyard still resembled a chessboard
set for a game.
Shortly the game would start
between the darkness and the first red dawn.

The Moon, that lovely lady,
was behind our backs that night.
She belonged to the romantic poets
and her beauty
was passed on by the dead to the living
like a gold ring.
She last belonged to Mácha.

Hora has long been dead,
he died young.
When spring comes
and in his garden in Hořín
the fruit trees burst into blossom
to remind us of the tender bloom
and brittleness of his verses
I hurry over to Vyšehrad, to the Hall of Fame.
I have a key.

Inside I knock at the plaque of the niche
with his name.
But there is the silence of the grave.
Only once did I think
I heard a soft sigh.

I still return to the places
I used to love,
and I feel as if I were stroking
an amorous fold of velvet.

I used to sit quite near the tomb
of the Passau Bishop Thun-Hohenstein,
who has been kneeling in the Little City cemetery,
hands folded,
these one hundred and fifty years.

Perhaps I wasn't there alone.
Indeed I wasn't,
when abruptly from the evening sky
a spring shower came down.
We sheltered in the Plague Chapel,
by the cemetery gate:
its door was shut
by the wind alone.

Through the cracked window the moonlight fell
into the chapel,
so palely brilliant, brilliantly pale,
illuminating a frightened face.
The light was cold
like a dead man's hand,
but the girl's lips were hot
and tasted of raindrops
At that moment there wasn't anything more beautiful
in all the world.

My Lord Bishop, pray
for me too!

The changes that have taken place
in those few years!
The chapel has long been pulled down
and rain no longer falls for me
at intimate moments
Even the Moon who now tiptoes
into the rectangle of my window
is no longer the same.

The moment when a human foot
first stepped on her
she was already dead.
She's died a few minutes earlier,
as soon as men with their instruments
began to float down on
her cold nakedness.

What we now see in the sky
is just a dead satellite,
and the jaws of its craters
chew upon nothingness.

Her ripped-off rose-red veils
she drags across the sky
and treads on them in the heavenly mud.

She continues orbiting the Earth,
but without any real meaning now,
as at the creation of the world,
complete with all that ironmongery
left behind
by the happy Americans.

THE HEAD OF THE VIRGIN MARY

It is a unique moment every year.
I opened the window, the curtains grated,
and autumn was here.
A silky one at that, with little drops of blood
and a light touch of sadness.
That is the time when human wounds
begin to hurt more.
I went to see Vladimír Holan.
He was ill.

He lived near the Lužice Seminary,
almost above the river.
The sun had just set behind the houses,
the river was rustling softly,
shuffling its wet cards into the evening's game.

As soon as I had entered
Holan snapped his book shut
and asked me almost angrily
if I too believed,
if I believed in life after death
or in something even worse.

But I ignored his words.
On the low cabinet by the door
I caught sight of the cast of a female head.
Good Lord, I know that one!
It was lying there, resting upon its face
as if under the guillotine.

It was the head of the Virgin Mary
from the Old City Square.
It had been toppled by pilgrims
when exactly sixty years ago
they returned from the White Mountain.

They overturned the column with the four armed angels
on which she stood.
It was nowhere as high
as the Vendôme in Paris.

May they be forgiven.
It towered there as a memento of defeat and shame
for the Czech nation
and the pilgrims were a little high
on the first breath of freedom.

I was there with them
and the head of the broken column
rolled over the pavement near
where I was standing.
When it came to a halt
her pious eyes were gazing
upon my dusty boots.

Now it came rolling up to me
A second time.
Between those two moments lay
almost a whole human life
that was my own.
I'm not saying it was happy
but it is now at an end.

\- Do tell me again what it was
you asked me as I entered.
And do forgive me.

FOUR SMALL WINDOWS

If a stranger asked me
what spot in Prague I was fondest of
I'd say without hesitation:
The New Stairway up to the Castle.
And just to myself I'd add:
And the little garden of the sculptress Wichterlová
on the flank of Petřín Hill.

I listened to a waterfall there
under the vault of a hydrangea.
It was a small one and its song was soft,
the gentle song of water.
Yet at nightfall its voice was more moving
than the song of the nightingale out there
under the vault of the stars.

Stairs compel us not to stay below
but to climb higher.
Up top there's always some surprise.
But if on the stairs I hear behind me
the footfall of a boy,
then this is none other than myself,
myself aged fourteen.

Those four small tearful windows
in Jan Zrzavý's studio
look down on Prague
still full of mourning for the painter.
His palette now is cracked,
his brushes dried hard.

I called on him some years ago.
It was afternoon
and he was about to do some painting.

When he opened the first window
he would see the ancient Capuchin monastery
near Saint Loretto.
Outside the monastery there is an iron crucifix
and under it a bunch of lilac.
It was spring just then.

In his second window
he looked at some cottages at Okrouhlice,
where he was fond of going.
They were human and gentle, and somehow festive
as though on Corpus Christi.
A poor angel was picking wild flowers
on the edge of the corn.

In the third window stood the lighthouse
of Ile de la Seine.
Autumn was clearly approaching
and the lighthouse shone on fishermen's houses
disdainfully turning their backs
on the sea.

In the last window, finally,
was the column and Ducal Palace
and behind it the domes of Saint Mark's.
They were rose-coloured and golden.
But, for heaven's sake, where is that flock of pigeons
making for from the Palace of the Doge?
They're settling in the Little City Square,
where many cars are parked,
and amidst the dusting of snow are pecking grains
which smell of petrol.

When the painter had closed the window
he got down to work.

As a boy I'd sit on the steps
under the Castle wall
and concupiscently watch
the girls' legs
hurrying past unconcernedly
and foolish desires rocked
my senses.
But I was still afraid of love.

Until one day someone leaned over to me,
I've no idea who it was,
and quietly said to my face:
What are you afraid of? Get up
and go!

The Seminary Garden was seething with flowers,
enough to make your eyes brim over,
and the viewing tower above it
was not yet then of iron.
It looked more like a delicate dragonfly
hovering in the air
with wings so transparent
they can't be seen.

And I obeyed, got up
and went.

A VISIT TO THE PAINTER VLADIMÍR KOMÁREK

Into the birdsong I'd called out en route:
Long live painting!
That vertigo of the eyes,
that perpetual unrest of the blood.
Shyly I knocked, the door was open.

I caught sight first of a familiar basket.
It was pink.
In it the painter had once painted
half a dozen young doves.
But in the window flew a strip of lace
torn off the Eiffel Tower.

Long live Paris! I said to myself silently.
That city throws up new images,
one image after another,
as a queen bee after her wedding flight
its eggs.
Does Paris ever sleep?
And the buzz of the beehive is a waterfall
heard from afar.

But here is silence. The bats quietly
hang by their claws on all four sides,
heads downward.
Only at times does an old cupboard creak
with nostalgia
for what things used to be.
Meanwhile the painter started to explain:

If I should ever have to paint a nude
and there the girl was waiting by the easel,
just as a patient in a surgery
waits for the silver acupuncture needles,
perhaps I'd rather paint
the quiet sadness of the things
which are all round us here
than the girl's living skin,
in whose sweet hues as in a fountain
spring washes its impatient eyes.

In the outlines of the things on which I look
I paint what the eye does not see.
And that is art.

But as a fisherman draws from a living fish
transparent sparks,
I force from things, if need be by brute force,
their tears.
And that is poetry.

As I was getting ready to depart
and it was getting late
I asked Mr Komárek
to show me the way
from his pastel landscapes
to the bus stop.

Go down the stairs,
and cross the bridge,
but only half-way,
until you find yourself in the trees' little clouds.
And if you like the grey of pigeons
you'll stand in front of Notre-Dame.

AN UMBRELLA FROM PICCADILLY

If you're at your wits' end with love
try falling in love again –
say, with the Queen of England.
Why not?
Her features are on every postage stamp
of that ancient kingdom.
But if you were to ask her
for a date in Hyde Park
you can bet on it
you'd wait in vain.

If you've any sense at all
you'll wisely tell yourself:
Why of course, I know:
it's raining in Hyde Park today.

When he was coming back from England
my son bought me in London's Piccadilly
an elegant umbrella.
Whenever necessary
I now have above my head
my own small sky
which may be black
but in its tensioned wire spokes
God's mercy may be flowing like
electric current.

I open my umbrella even when it's not raining,
as a canopy
over the volume of Shakespeare's sonnets
I carry with me in my pocket.

But there are moments when I am frightened
even by the sparkling bouquet of the universe.
Outstripping its beauty
it threatens us with its infinity
and that is all too similar
to the sleep of death.

It also threatens us with the void and frostiness
of its thousands of stars
which at night delude us
with their gleam.

The one we have named Venus
is downright terrifying.
Its rocks are still on the boil
and like gigantic waves of the sea
mountains are rising up
and burning sulphur falls.

We always ask where hell is.
It is there!

But what use is a fragile umbrella
against the universe?
Besides I don't even carry it.
I have enough of a job
to walk along,
clinging close to the ground
as a nocturnal moth in daytime
to the coarse bark of a tree.

All my life I have sought the paradise
that used to be here,
whose traces I have found
only on women's lips
and in the curves of their skin
when it was warm with love.

All my life I've longed
for freedom.
At last I've discovered the door
that leads to it.
It is death.

Now that I'm old
some charming woman's face
will sometimes waft between my lashes
and her smile will stir my blood.

Shyly I turn my head
and remember the Queen of England
whose features are on every postage stamp
of that ancient kingdom.
God save the Queen!

Oh yes, I know quite well:
it's raining in Hyde Park today.

THE STRUGGLE WITH THE ANGEL

God knows who first thought up
that gloomy image
and spoke of the dead
as of living shades
straying about amongst us.

And yet these shades are really here –
you can't not see them.
All my life I've had around me
a numerous cluster.
But it is I amidst them all
that's straying.

They're dark
and they are mute in time
with my own muteness
when the evening's closing in
and I'm alone.
Only now and again they stay my writing hand,
when I'm not right,
and blow away an evil thought
that's painful.

Some of them are so dim
and faded
I'm losing sight of them in the far distance.

One of the shades, however, is rose-red:
it's sleeping.
In every person's life
there comes a moment
when everything suddenly goes black before his eyes
and he longs passionately to embrace
a smiling head.
His heart wants to be tied
to another heart,
even by deep stitches,
while his lips desire nothing more
than to touch down on the spots where
the midnight raven settled on Pallas Athene,
when uninvited it flew in to visit
a melancholy poet.

It is called love.
All right!
Perhaps that's what it is.
But only rarely does it last for long,
let alone unto death
as in the case of swans.
Often loves succeed each other
like suits of cards in your hand.

Sometime's it's just a tremor of delight,
more often long and bitter pain.
At other times all sighs and tears.
And sometimes even boredom.
That's the saddest kind.

Some time in the past I saw a rose-red shade.
It stood by the entrance to a house
whose façade was facing
Prague's railway station,
eternally swathed in smoke.

We used to sit there by the window.
I held her delicate hands
and talked of love.
I'm good at that!
She's long been dead.
The red lights were winking
down by the track.

As soon as the wind sprang up a little
it blew away the grey veil
and the rails were glistening
like the strings of some fabulous piano.

At times you could also hear the whistle of steam
and the puffing of the engines
as they carried off people's wretched longings
from the grimy platforms
to all corners of the earth.
Sometimes they also carry the dead
returning to their homes
and to their cemeteries.

Now I know why it hurts so
to tear hand from hand,
lips from lips,
when the stitches tear
and the guard slams shut
the last carriage door.

Love's an eternal struggle with the angel.
From dawn to night.
And without mercy.
The opponent is often stronger.
But woe to him
who doesn't realize
that his angel has no wings
and will not bless.

FRAGMENT OF A LETTER

All night the rain lashed the windows.
I couldn't go to sleep.
So I switched on the light
and wrote a letter.

If love could fly,
as of course it can't,
and didn't so often stay close to the ground,
it would be delightful to be enveloped
in its breeze.

But like infuriated bees
jealous kisses swarm down upon
the sweetness of the female body
and an impatient hand grasps
whatever it can reach,
and desire does not flag.
Even death might be without terror
at the moment of exultation.

But who has ever calculated
how much love goes
into one pair of open arms!

Letters to women
I always sent by pigeon post.
My conscience is clear.
I never entrusted them to sparrowhawks
or goshawks.

Under my pen the verses dance no longer
and like a tear in the corner of the eye
the word hangs back.
And all my life at its end
is now only a fast journey on a train:

I'm standing by the window of the carriage
and day after day
speeds back into yesterday
to join the black mists of sorrow.
At times I helplessly catch hold
of the emergency brake.

Perhaps I shall once more catch sight
of a woman's smile,
trapped like a torn-off flower
on the lashes of her eyes.
Perhaps I may still be allowed
to send those eyes at least one kiss
before they're lost to me in the dark.

Perhaps once more I shall even see
a slender ankle
chiselled like a gem
from warm tenderness,
so that I might once more
half-choke with longing.

How much is there that man must leave behind
as the train inexorably approaches
Lethe station
with its plantations of shimmering asphodels
amidst whose perfumes everything is forgotten.
Including human love.

But that is then the final stop:
the train goes no further.

WINDOW ON BIRDS' WINGS

Even water, infused with lilies-of-the-valley,
is poisonous.
How much more so is spring!
It penetrates into the living tissue
like a neutron bomb
and infects everything alive.
Only the stone stays motionless.
At most it may slightly change
the surly colour of its face.

I hastened past the plates
with the street names,
nailed only to the spring breeze.
I was hurrying towards the only window,
dazzlingly blue.
The birds were bearing it to me
on their wings.
Each day a little closer.

And then my window shut.
Yet sometimes I see it
but only if I close my eyes . . .
And yesterday came autumn.

The grapes are golden tassels
on the curtain
of an amateur dramatic society
and the silence that goes with autumn
speaks in the mother tongue of cemeteries,
where gradually the runnels of our lives
converge.

Pain I know well,
it is an evil and an obstinate sister.
Death is a mystery
paid for by horror.
The window has long been demolished,
the birds have flown off to the vineyards.

To listen to the silence one more moment,
when the eyes believe
that the full grapes on the bush
long to be grasped.
Man reaches out for love
and woman shrieks with pleasure . . .

Below the vineyard flows the ancient river,
and while the breeze is playing
with the rustling leaves
the river carries off
all the sweet waters of this country
into the dirty sea at Hamburg.

THE MISTRESS OF THE POETS

Those foolish moments of first love!
I still believed then that
to die amidst spring blossom
if you are in love
head over heels,
or to die at the Venice carnival,
can be more beautiful
than in bed at home.

But death is the lady of all pains
known to the world.
Her train is woven
from the rattle in the throat of the dying
and embroidered with the stars of tears.

Death is the lute of lamentations,
the torch of burning blood,
the urn of love
and the door to nowhere.

Sometimes death is the mistress of the poets.
Let them court her
in the stench of dead flowers,
if they can bear
the tolling of the gloomy bells
which are now on the march,
stamping though bloody mud.

70

Death slips into the female body
with its long narrow hand
and chokes the infants under the heart.
True, they may go to paradise,
but still all bloody.

Death is the empress of all killing
and her sceptre
has from the origin of the world
commanded the horrors of war . . .

Death is the younger sister of decay,
the messenger of ruin and nothingness
and her hands
push upon everybody's breast
the burden of the grave.

But death is also just an instant,
a scratching of the pen
and no more.

LOST PARADISE

The Old Jewish Cemetery
is one great bouquet of grey stone
on which time has trodden.
I was drifting among the graves,
thinking of my mother.
She used to read the Bible.

The letters in two columns
welled up before her eyes
like blood from a wound.
The lamp was guttering and smoking
and Mother put on her glasses.
At times she had to blow it out
and with her hairpin straighten
the glowing wick.

But when she closed her tired eyes
she dreamed of Paradise,
before God had garrisoned it
with armed cherubim . . .
Often she fell asleep over the Book
which slipped from her lap.

I was still young
when I discovered in the Old Testament
those fascinating verses about love
and eagerly searched for
the passages on incest . . .
That time I did not yet suspect
how much tenderness is hidden in the names
of Old Testament women.

Adah is Ornament and Orpah
is a Hind,
Naamah is the Pleasant
and Nikol the Little Brook.
Abigail is the Fount of Exultation.

But if I recall how helplessly I watched
as they dragged off the Jews,
even the crying children,
I still shudder with horror
and a chill runs down my spine.

Jemima is the Dove and Tamar
a Palm Tree.
Tirzah is Pleasantness
and Zilpah a Raindrop.
My God, how beautiful this is!

We were living in hell
yet no one dared to strike the weapon
from the murderers' hands.
As if within our hearts we did not have
a spark of humanity!

The name Jecholiah means
The Lord is Mighty.
And yet their frowning God
gazed over the barbed wire
and did not move a finger –

Delilah is the Delicate, Rachel
the Little Ewe,
Deborah the Bee
and Esther the Bright Star.

I'd just returned from the cemetery
when the June wind with its scents
leaned against the windows.
But from the silent distance now and then came thunder
of a future war.
There is no time without murder.

I should like to forget.
Rhoda is the Rose.
And this flower perhaps is the only thing
that's left to us on earth
from ancient Paradise.

THE ROYAL PAVILION

The times I've walked through southern pine groves
under the sun of Tuscany
and wandered along ruined walls
and scattered dried-up wells
over whose crumbling sides
ivy was creeping.

The times I've sat gazing,
on the benches of ancient cathedrals
and before altars, at those famous women
whose heads were garlanded
with the verses of poets
and whose beauty sat like a jewel
on the breast of Italy.

Today I am too old –
but neither in memories nor in dreams
do legs get tired.

Last night there was a full moon.
In the Chotek Gardens
it was as light as day
and lovers were trying in vain
to conceal their kisses.

On the white foreheads of the marble statues
by the small grotto
the moonlight fell that night,
and the faces, normally so gentle,
were frightening
like the faces of the dead
rising from their graves.

The fountain fell silent, the water was slumbering
and the delicate bellies of a thousand droplets
ceased to beat against the wet metal.
Only the small fieldmice
under the fountain
were scurrying about the garden flowers
as in a maze.

Today someone will raise the torch
which tints the roofs green
to light the path, when the dance is ended,
for the girl dancers' weary feet –
just a few steps.

When they had all gone
the columns in the empty arcades moved off
and like mute pilgrims
set out on their pilgrimage.
They walked without heads
and without legs and without arms
and without rosaries,
with only their broken shadows
all about the pavilion.

76

At that moment the curtains across the sky
abruptly parted
and before my eyes appeared the Cathedral
and below it the Castle
with all the towers of the ancient battlements.

Whenever I gaze out on Prague
– and I do so constantly and always with bated breath
because I love her –
I turn my mind to God
wherever he may hide from me,
beyond the starry mists
or just behind that moth-eaten screen,
to thank him
for granting me that magnificent setting
to live in.
To me and to my joys and carefree loves,
to me and to my tears without weeping
when the loves departed,
and to my more-than-bitter grief
when even my verses could not weep.
I love her fire-charred walls
to which we clung during the war
so as to hold out.
I would not change them for anything in the world.
Not even for others,
not even if the Eiffel Tower rose between them
and the Seine flowed sadly past,
not even for all the gardens of paradise
full of flowers.

When I shall die – and this will be quite soon –
I shall still carry in my heart
this city's destiny.

And mercilessly, just as Marsyas,
let anyone be flayed alive
who lays hands on this city,
no matter who he is.
No matter how sweetly he plays
on his flute.

A BOWL OF NUTS

I've long got used to not hearing,
here and there,
the Flower Song from Carmen,
and the wind is throwing snow into my eyes
so I shouldn't see
what lies close before me.

On Christmas Day I place at the table
an extra three chairs.
One for my dead father,
the second for my mother,
and this year a third for my sister.
She was killed in a car.

Sometimes I'm also visited by others
whom I loved in this life.
They are curious.
As I slice my apple
they peer over my shoulder.

This always is a precious moment in the year
for tears of remembrance.
But we won't let the sirens on the roofs
sob and wail
as at the beginning of May.
We'll cry quietly, alone.

But what can I set before them,
what can I offer my ghosts?
Here is the bread of this country
and its rough wine,
here is a bowl of cashew nuts
from far away, from India,
and they taste sweet
like the first childish kisses.

Maybe these words
will make my mother smile.
But I'm not sure.
She used to smile with her lips alone,
her eyes were permanently sad.

And when she wept
her tears flowed inward.